SHANNON

WE ARE STILL HERE

NATIVE AMERICANS TODAY

SHANNON

An Ojibway Dancer

Sandra King

Photographs by Catherine Whipple
With a Foreword by Michael Dorris

Lerner Publications Company ● Minneapolis

Series Editor: Gordon Regguinti
Series Consultants: W. Roger Buffalohead, Juanita G. Corbine Espinosa
Illustrations by Carly Bordeau. The floral illustrations are based on Ojibway
   beadwork designs.
Photographs on pages 25, 36, and 37 by Susan Braine.
Photographs on pages 40 and 44 by Dale Kakkak.

This book is available in two editions:
Library binding by Lerner Publications Company
Soft cover by First Avenue Editions
241 First Avenue North
Minneapolis, MN 55401

ISBN: 0-8225-2652-2 (lib. bdg.)
ISBN: 0-8225-9643-1 (pbk.)

LIBRARY OF CONGRESS CATALOGING-IN-PUBLICATION DATA

King, Sandra.
   Shannon, an Ojibway dancer / Sandra King : photographs by
Catherine Whipple : with a foreword by Michael Dorris.
      p.   cm. — (We are still here)
   Includes bibliographical references.
   Summary: A thirteen-year-old Ojibwa Indian living in Minneapolis,
Minnesota, learns about her tribe's traditional costumes from her
grandmother and gets ready to dance at a powwow.
   ISBN 0-8225-2652-2 (lib. bdg.)
   1. Ojibwa Indians—Dances—Juvenile literature. 2. Powwows—
Minnesota—Minneapolis—Juvenile literature. 3. Ojibwa Indians—
Rites and ceremonies—Juvenile literature. [1. Ojibwa Indians—
Dances. 2. Indians of North America—Minnesota—Dances. 3. Ojibwa
Indians—Costume and adornment 4. Indians of North America—
Minnesota—Costume and adornment 5. Powwows.] I. Whipple,
Catherine, ill. II. Title III. Series
E99.C6K54   1993
394'.3—dc20   92-27261
                                                      CIP
                                                       AC

Manufactured in the United States of America

1 2 3 4 5 6 – P/JR – 98 97 96 95 94 93

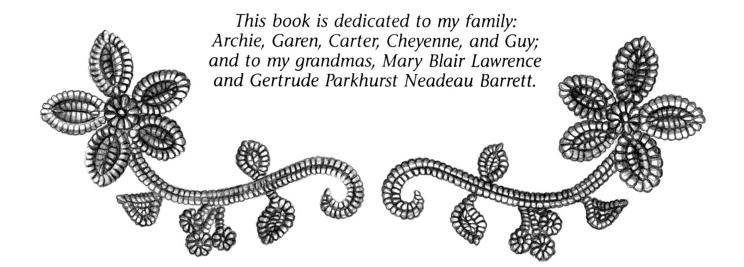

This book is dedicated to my family:
Archie, Garen, Carter, Cheyenne, and Guy;
and to my grandmas, Mary Blair Lawrence
and Gertrude Parkhurst Neadeau Barrett.

Foreword

by Michael Dorris

How do we get to be who we are? What are the ingredients that shape our values, customs, language, and tastes, that bond us into a unit different from any other? On a large scale, what makes the Swedes Swedish or the Japanese Japanese?

These questions become even more subtle and interesting when they're addressed to distinct and enduring traditional cultures coexisting within the boundaries of a large and complex society. Certainly Americans visiting abroad have no trouble recognizing their fellow countrymen and women, be they black or white, descended from Mexican or Polish ancestors, rich or poor. As a people, we have much in common, a great deal that we more or less share: a recent history, a language, a common denominator of popular music, entertainment, and politics.

But, if we are fortunate, we also belong to a small, more particular community, defined by ethnicity or kinship, belief system or geography. It is in this intimate circle that we are most "ourselves," where our jokes are best appreciated, our special dishes most enjoyed. These are the people to whom we go first when we need comfort or empathy, for they speak our own brand of cultural shorthand, and always know the correct things to say, the proper things to do.

Shannon provides an insider's view into just such a world, that of the contemporary Ojibway people. If we are ourselves Ojibway, we will probably nod often while reading these pages, affirming the familiar, approving that this tribal family keeps alive and passes on the traditions of beadwork and dance. If we belong to another tribe, we will follow Shannon's story with interest, gaining respect for a way of doing things that's rich and rewarding.

This is a book about people who are neither exotic nor unusual. If you encountered them at a shopping mall or at a movie theater they might seem at first glance like everyone else, a grandmother and her grandchildren, American as apple pie. *Shannon* does not dispute this picture, but it does expand it.

Michael Dorris is the author of *A Yellow Raft in Blue Water, The Broken Cord,* and, with Louise Erdrich, *The Crown of Columbus.* His first book for children is *Morning Girl.*

S hannon hurried home from school. She planned to go to the mall this afternoon with Kaitlin and Contessa. It was always fun to go someplace with them. They were two of her best friends.

Grandma wasn't home from work yet when Shannon got there. But her cousin Chantelle was sitting at the table with a pencil and paper. "Come here," she said to Shannon. "Tell me if you like this design."

Shannon looked over Chantelle's shoulder. The design was of flowers, leaves, and hearts. "Nicole drew it," Chantelle said. "It's for a new outfit. We're almost finished with the orange outfit, so we can start this one real soon."

Shannon and Chantelle enjoy designing beadwork for their dance outfits.

Chantelle, Candace, and Shannon in front of their house

Shannon Anderson is Ojibway. She lives in Minneapolis, Minnesota, with her grandma, Mary Jane Anderson, and her sisters, Nicole and Candace. Nicole, 15, is the oldest. Shannon is 13 and Candace is 12. Shannon's cousins, Bruce and Chantelle, also live with them. Bruce is 9 and Chantelle is 11.

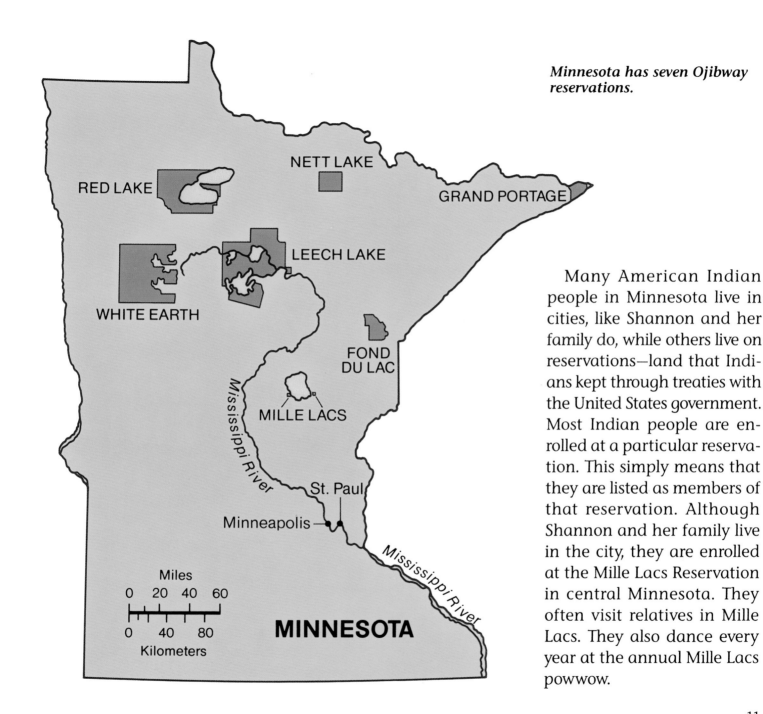

Minnesota has seven Ojibway reservations.

RED LAKE

NETT LAKE

GRAND PORTAGE

LEECH LAKE

WHITE EARTH

FOND DU LAC

Mississippi River

MILLE LACS

St. Paul

Minneapolis

Mississippi River

Miles

0   20   40   60

0   40   80

Kilometers

MINNESOTA

Many American Indian people in Minnesota live in cities, like Shannon and her family do, while others live on reservations—land that Indians kept through treaties with the United States government. Most Indian people are enrolled at a particular reservation. This simply means that they are listed as members of that reservation. Although Shannon and her family live in the city, they are enrolled at the Mille Lacs Reservation in central Minnesota. They often visit relatives in Mille Lacs. They also dance every year at the annual Mille Lacs powwow.

11

Shannon and Nicole are fancy shawl dancers. Fancy shawl is a vigorous dance in which a dancer uses intricate, or "fancy," footwork, and twirls the shawl that she wears. Candace and Chantelle are jingle dress dancers. A jingle dress, covered with small metal cones, makes a jingling sound as the dancer moves. Shannon, her sisters, and her cousins dance at pow-wows all across Minnesota. They also travel to Wisconsin, North and South Dakota, and Canada to dance.

Shannon in her fancy shawl outfit and Chantelle in her jingle dress

Powwows are traditional Indian social events that feature drumming and dancing. They take place all over the United States and Canada throughout the year. They are held in cities and on reservations, indoors and outdoors, in winter and summer. Summer, though, is considered powwow season. Some reservations have held powwows for more than 100 years.

Candace, Shannon, and Chantelle take a break from dancing at the Mille Lacs powwow.

Shannon hoped that the outfit she and her cousin were working on would be ready in time for this year's Mille Lacs powwow. "I just have to finish the moccasins," Shannon told Chantelle.

Shannon took one of the moccasins from her sewing basket and set to work. She threaded a long beading needle with beading thread and then pulled the thread twice through a small cake of beeswax. The wax waterproofed the thread and would help make the beadwork strong. Shannon tied a knot at the end of the thread and began where she had left off the day before. She was working on the moccasin's background, sewing in rows of brown beads. Her grandma showed her how to do this a long time ago, when Shannon was about seven.

Shannon poked the needle through the fabric and then picked up five brown beads on her needle. She pushed the beads to the end of the thread and laid them next to the last five beads she had sewn down. Then she put her needle in the material again and pulled it through. The rows of beads fit snugly together. Now she went back and made a small stitch between every two beads in the new row. Shannon was proud of the way her beadwork lay flat and smooth.

Shannon beaded the moccasin until her grandma came home from work. By that time, everyone else was home, too. The roast that Nicole had put in the oven was beginning to smell very good. Shannon likes venison. She knew Grandma would save her a slice to eat after she got home from the mall.

Left: *Kaitlin, Contessa, and Shannon at the mall.* Below: *Shannon fixes Kaitlin's hair.*

Grandma drove Shannon and her friends to Har Mar Mall in St. Paul and dropped them off. Kaitlin's dad would pick them up in two hours. Shannon, Kaitlin, and Contessa love browsing at the mall. They visited every shop they could, spending a lot of time at the shoe store. They made a side trip to the restroom and fixed Kaitlin's hair in front of the big mirror there. Then they were off to the video games.

17

Shannon and Contessa play video games.

Shannon's favorite game is Pac-Man. Her friends sometimes tease her about liking such an old game, but Shannon loves to watch Pac-Man chomp his way through the maze. She feels loyal to him. Kaitlin and Contessa like the race car games. They all enjoy playing Ninja Turtles.

"This Turtle game is fun," Shannon said. "Even though we never get anywhere." They all laughed and played the game again.

Shannon had met Kaitlin in the second grade and Contessa in the fourth grade. They had all gone to Northrup School together through the sixth grade. Now Shannon goes to a different school, but she still likes to spend time with her old friends whenever she can.

18

Shannon's new school, called Four Winds School, has an American Indian and French language immersion program. "Immersion" means that the students learn an Indian language or the French language by being immersed in the language, or totally plunged into it. During the whole class period, teachers and students speak only the language they are studying.

Shannon in school, with her classmates and teacher

This semester Shannon is taking English, French, social studies, math, gym, and science. Next semester she will take an Ojibway language class. Four Winds School offers several courses that are of special interest to American Indian students. It also has many Native American teachers. Not all the students at this school are Indian, but most of them are.

In addition to Four Winds, a public school, there are several private schools in the city where students can study Indian culture. A public school in St. Paul also offers Indian studies. Now young Indian students in Minneapolis and St. Paul can choose from many different schools where they can study American Indian languages and cultures.

When Shannon got home from the mall that evening, she found two slices of venison on a plate in the refrigerator. Grandma had saved it for her just like Shannon knew she would. Shannon fixed a venison sandwich and sat down at the table by her grandma.

"You've done good work, my girl," Grandma said. She held up the moccasin Shannon had beaded.

"Thank you," Shannon said.

"Don't forget to sew in a mistake so that it isn't perfect," Grandma told her.

Shannon knew that most Ojibway beadwork contains one on-purpose mistake. Grandma says it is meant to keep the beadworker from false pride. Shannon's aunt Sandy once told Shannon that the on-purpose mistake was a sort of doorway for the spirit of whatever was being made. "Why would the spirit need a door?" Shannon had asked. "Perhaps it might want to leave," Aunt Sandy answered.

"Nicole is making a design for another new outfit," Shannon told her grandma. "Did you see it?"

"Yes, I did," Grandma said. "It's pretty. Maybe we can go shopping for beads tomorrow." Sometimes they order beads from a catalog. But Shannon likes it best when they go to one of the Indian stores and choose beads from the many looped bundles of colors hanging on the walls.

"Do you have homework?" Grandma asked.

"No, I don't. I think I'll work on these moccasins for a while."

When Shannon was finished with this last moccasin, the orange outfit would be complete.

Colorful beads and paintings line a wall at the Bear-Hawk Indian Store, where Shannon sometimes shops.

Shannon's dance group performs in downtown Minneapolis.

A fancy shawl dancer's outfit is very beautiful. Many different pieces are needed to complete an outfit: a dress, a shawl, a cape, leggings, moccasins, and a belt.

The shawl drapes over a dancer's shoulders and reaches to her fingertips across her outstretched arms. It usually hangs to just above her knee. Long fringe falls from the edges of the shawl. The fringe looks very pretty as it flies out and around the dancer when she twirls.

Some shawls are lined with silk or lace. Other shawls are plain or have cloth designs called appliqués sewn on them. Some are even painted with pictures of eagles, feathers, or flowers. A dancer chooses her own colors for the cloth and the fringe. Sometimes she uses the same colors for both, but most of the time the cloth and fringe contrast.

This dancer's shawl is decorated with ribbons and appliqués.

Shannon's grandma helps her make her shawls. First she sews a narrow hem around each side of the cloth. Then she puts on the fringe. There are different kinds of fringe. Shoe-string fringe is flat and wide. Some shawls are fringed with ribbon. Grandma likes to use silky strand fringe.

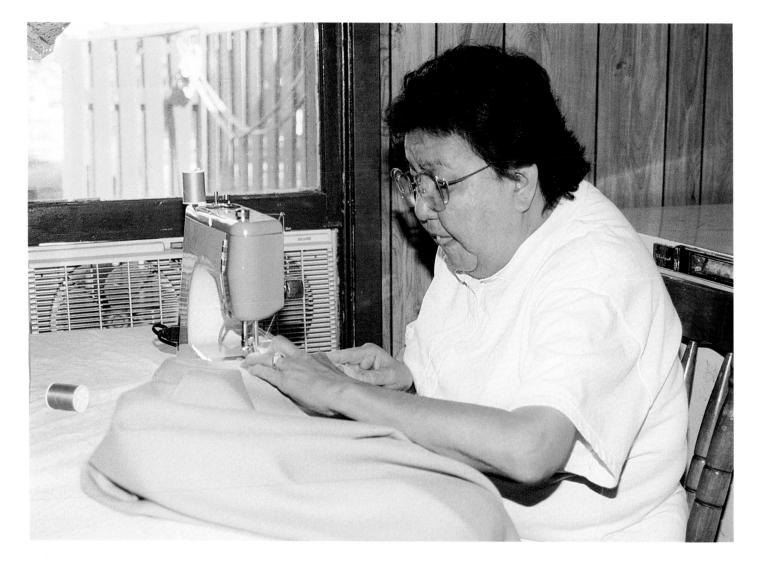

Shannon and Nicole repair their own shawls.

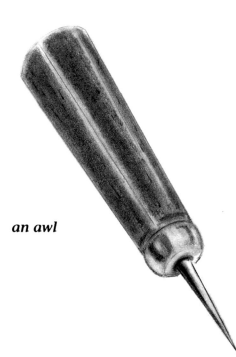

an awl

Strand fringe comes in a roll. Grandma cuts it into lengths before she uses it. Then she attaches the fringe to the cloth using a crochet hook and a pointed tool called an awl. First she pokes a hole in the cloth with the awl. Then she pushes the crochet hook through the hole and catches several strands of fringe on the hook. Grandma usually uses three strands, but some dancers make shawls with up to six strands of fringe in a hole. The crochet hook catches the strands in their middles, and Grandma pulls them through the hole in the cloth, making a small loop. Then she pulls the bottom part of the fringe through this loop and ties it into a smooth knot. She ties the fringe all the way around the shawl. It takes many hours of careful work to fringe one shawl.

Left: *Shannon wears her orange cape with her black shawl.* Center: *Shannon's leggings and moccasins.* Below: *She also has a matching cape and belt.*

The cape, also called a cowl, fits over a dancer's head and lays over the shawl. Capes are often made of beads, like both of Shannon's are. Capes can be made of beads, sequins, cloth, or combinations of all three.

Leggings are like cloth boots without feet. They fit around a dancer's legs and are decorated to match her cape.

The moccasins are often beaded, too. Some dancers sew sequins on their moccasins to match a flashy cape and legging combination.

The dancer's belt might also match her cape and leggings, although most dancers have one all-purpose belt that goes with many dance outfits.

A fancy shawl dancer usually wears her hair in two braids. To these she attaches beaded hair ties and long cloth or fur extensions. She may also tie long strands of ribbon, in colors that match her outfit, to her hair ties.

If a dancer receives an eagle feather from an elder or a war veteran, she can wear it while she dances. Shannon's eagle feather was given to her by a man from the Red Lake Reservation when she was eight. He is a dancer whom Shannon often sees at powwows.

Shannon wears her eagle feather at powwows.

"What colors do you think we should make the new outfit, Grandma?" Shannon asked. She was finished with her venison sandwich and thought a glass of milk would taste good.

Grandma smiled. "Whatever you choose, my girl. I hope we finish it in time for the Mille Lacs powwow this year, don't you?"

"We can. Aunt Sandy will help." Shannon's aunt Sandy helps with all the girls' dance outfits. She does most of the beadwork, and Grandma makes the shawls, dresses, and jingle dresses.

Shannon put one last row of beads on the moccasins, drank a glass of milk, and went to bed.

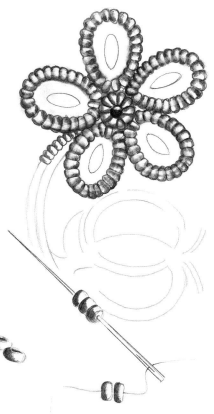

Franklin Avenue runs through Shannon's Minneapolis neighborhood.

*T*he next day, Grandma, Shannon, Nicole, Candace, and Chantelle all went shopping to buy new beads. They walked down Franklin Avenue, through their neighborhood on the south side of Minneapolis. Sometimes Shannon and Grandma see their friends out shopping, too, and they stop to visit. Many Indian people live in this neighborhood. The Minneapolis American Indian Center, where Grandma works as a job counselor, is also here.

31

The Minneapolis American Indian Center contains offices, a gym, a kitchen, a lecture hall, an art gallery, and two stores. The stores sell beadwork, silver jewelry, beads and needles, powwow music tapes, books, posters, and clothing. The center also publishes a newspaper for Indian people.

Minneapolis is not the only city with an Indian center. St. Paul, Chicago, Denver, and other cities have centers where Indian people can come for various services and programs. The Indian center in Minneapolis sponsors programs in education, the arts, recreation, housing, jobs, and child welfare.

Grandma at work at the Minneapolis American Indian Center

Finally Shannon and her family reached the Bear-Hawk Indian Store, farther down Franklin Avenue. They like this store with its good supply of beads in all sizes and colors. It also sells jewelry, shawls, ribbon shirts, and greeting cards. After about half an hour, they made up their minds. They decided to put the new design on a pale blue background.

"Maybe we should buy some extra orange and brown beads too, in case I need to repair the moccasins," Shannon said. It is up to each dancer to keep her moccasins in good repair.

Shopping for beads at the Bear-Hawk Indian Store

Shannon began dancing when she was just two years old. She thinks she probably learned to dance the way she sees other little kids learn—they just go out and dance. The more they dance, the better they become. Later, when they get the hang of it, an older dancer will show them the harder steps and coach them as they practice. Shannon's sister Nicole is her coach.

Shannon sometimes helps younger children learn to dance.

Shannon, Nicole, and Candace get dressed for a powwow.

Shannon belongs to two drum and dance groups—one called Two Rivers, and another sponsored by the Minneapolis Indian Health Board. She and her sisters usually practice once a week. But just before a powwow, Nicole gets them all to practice for three days straight. They practice to music, learning the different songs, so that they can dance with the beat and be sure to stop on time. It's always fun dancing in the living room with the powwow tapes blasting and everyone laughing. Grandma tries to come home from work early on these practice days. She likes to watch.

group members sing in an Indian language, but sometimes they sing in English. When you hear these songs for the first time, they might all sound alike. But they are not. Each song has its own melody and words. Some songs honor the United States flag and others honor certain people. Some songs are played for specific dances, such as a fancy shawl or a jingle dress dance.

People say that the drum is the heart of the Indian people. Drumming is certainly the heart of every powwow. A group of singers and their drum are called a drum group.

Usually about 10 to 15 singers form a group.

Drum groups sing thousands of different songs at powwows across the country. Most of the time, the drum

Many dancers take part in powwows. People of all ages dance, from toddlers to elders. In this part of the country—around the Great Lakes—there are several different kinds of dances at a powwow. The boys' or men's traditional dance tells either the creation story or a story of a battle or hunt. The dancer acts out his story as he dances. The men's grass dance, with its graceful, flowing movements, shows men readying a campsite by tamping down the grass with their feet. Some say the dance depicts the movement of the grass itself. Another young men's dance is the fancy bustle—a very fast, acrobatic dance. Fancy dancers wear brightly colored outfits with feather bustles on the back.

Besides the fancy shawl and jingle dress dances, women and girls have a traditional powwow dance. It is slow and stately.

Candace, Chantelle, and Shannon wait their turn to dance.

Most powwows run for about three days. They are held over a weekend or long holiday so that people won't have to take time off from work or school. There are two basic kinds of powwows: contest and traditional.

A contest powwow is a little like the Olympic Games. Contestants dance in front of judges who award them points based on their skill. At the end of the powwow, the winners are announced along with the runners-up. Dance competition is not usually a part of the traditional powwow, but sometimes a family sponsors a small contest in honor of a loved one.

After they have finished dancing, Chantelle, Shannon, and Candace look at the powwow's craft displays.

Shannon likes both kinds of powwows. She is a good dancer, and she placed in contest powwows twice last year. This year she is especially looking forward to dancing in the Mille Lacs powwow. She likes visiting her cousins and seeing all her relatives there. She doesn't know them all. But she knows that anyone with the last name Pewaush, Gahbow, or Sam is her relation. At the Mille Lacs powwow, her family surrounds her. It feels good to dance there.

*A*t home that night, Shannon watched Grandma make the jingles for Candace's new dress. Grandma told her the story of how the first jingle dress was made. The jingle dress dance and dress appeared to an Ojibway woman in a dream, years ago. A loved one of hers, who was sick, was to wear the dress, dance, and be healed.

Jingle dresses come in all colors. Shiny silver-colored jingles hang across the front and back of the dancer's shoulders and in patterns around her skirt. A grown woman's jingle dress might have as many as 400 jingles. The jingles are made from thin metal, usually from snuff can lids. The lids are cut into a fan shape and then bent, or turned, into a cone shape. Short strips of cloth or ribbon are sewn to the dress about an inch apart and a knot is tied at the end of each strip. Then the jingle is slipped over the strip and pinched shut at the top, just above the knot. When a jingle dress dancer moves, the cones clink together and make a beautiful jingling sound.

Opposite: *Jingle dress dancers.* Below: *Snuff can lids, before and after they are turned into jingles.*

Shannon watched her grandma turn the jingles. Not many people know how to do this.

"Grandma, did you dance when you were little?"

"Oh, yes."

"What did you dance?"

"I was a jingle dress dancer, my girl. There were no fancy shawl dancers when I was little. That's something new. Go and put on that tape of pow-wow songs. We'll listen while we work."

42

The music filled the room. This tape was by the White-fish Bay drum group. It was Shannon's favorite.

"Boy, it's a good thing I'm Indian," Shannon said.

Grandma put her head back and laughed. "Now what makes you say that?" she asked.

"Oh, I don't know. I'm just glad that I dance. And that I see all my relatives at the Mille Lacs powwow. And my school has Indian teachers and . . . and my grandma makes jingle dresses!"

Grandma laughed again, but softly this time. "My girl," she said, "always remember to be glad. Remember that wherever you go, all that you are goes with you."

*I*ndian people have lived in the cities of Minneapolis and St. Paul for many years. During the Second World War, a large number of Indian people came to the cities to look for jobs. After the war ended, many of them stayed. And in the 1950s, even more Native Americans came from the reservations to look for jobs. Now half of all Indian people in Minnesota live in cities.

When Indian people meet each other for the first time, they say, "Where are you from?" They ask young people, "Who are your parents and grandparents? Where are they from?" Each Indian person belongs somewhere. Even though someone might have lived in a city for 50 years, that person will say he or she is from Mille Lacs, or Red Lake, or Rosebud, South Dakota.

Powwows are times for catching up with old friends.

A young person like Shannon, who was born in a city, also belongs. She holds a place in her tribe, among her relatives, and in a certain part of the Earth. This place belongs only to her and cannot be taken or given away. This is what Shannon's grandma meant when she told Shannon that wherever she goes, all that she is goes with her.

If you are in Mille Lacs at powwow time this year, look for Shannon. She'll be dancing.

Word List

appliqué—a cutout cloth design sewn onto another piece of fabric. Appliqués are often used to decorate shawls.

Dakota—American Indian people from the Great Plains; also called Sioux

elder—an older person who is respected and admired for his or her knowledge and experience

enrolled—to be listed as a member of a particular Indian reservation

fancy bustle—an energetic and acrobatic young men's dance. The dancer wears a colorful bustle made of feathers, around the waist and over the hips.

fancy shawl—a young women's dance of intricate footwork, spins, and twirls of the dancer's fringed shawl

grass dance—a boys' and men's dance with a graceful weaving, bobbing step

jingle dress—a girls' or women's dress covered with jingles, or the bouncing dance of a girl or woman wearing this dress

jingles—small cone-shaped pieces of metal

leggings—cloth or leather coverings worn on the legs

Ojibway—American Indian people from the Great Lakes area; also called Anishinabe or Chippewa

powwow—an American Indian social event featuring drum groups and dancers

reservations—areas of land that Indian people kept through treaties with the U.S. government

For Further Reading

Coombs, Linda. *Powwow.* Cleveland, Ohio: Modern Curriculum Press, Inc., 1991.

Goodchild, Peter. *The Spark in the Stone: Skills and Projects from the Native American Tradition.* Chicago: Chicago Review Press, 1991.

Lester, Joan A. *We're Still Here: Art of New England/The Children's Museum Collection.* Boston: The Children's Museum, 1987.

McIntosh, Chief W. E., and Harvey Shell. *Indian Craft.* Happy Camp, California: Naturegraph Publishers, Inc., 1987.

Stan, Susan. *The Ojibwe.* Vero Beach, Florida: Rourke Publications, Inc., 1989.

Tanner, Helen Hornbeck. Frank W. Porter III, gen. ed. *The Ojibwa.* New York: Chelsea House Pub., 1992.

About the Contributors

Sandra King is a member of the Red Lake band of Ojibway. She has edited various publications, including *The Circle*, an American Indian newspaper; *IKWE*, a monthly magazine for Indian students; *Strawberry Songs*, an anthology; and *Mini Sa*, a collection of works by Minnesota writers and artists. King lives with her husband, Archie, and their four children in St. Paul, Minnesota.

Catherine Whipple, Lakota, was born in South Dakota. She is a freelance photographer who serves on the board of directors for Native Arts Circle, a statewide Native American arts agency in Minnesota. Whipple received the 1991 McKnight Photography Fellowship for her work photographing working children in Central America. "As a Native American photographer," Whipple says, "I believe it is necessary to document our social and political lives from our own perspective. It is important that we reclaim our own images, and that we have control over the way we are portrayed to the rest of the world." Whipple lives in Minneapolis.

Illustrator **Carly Bordeau** is a member of the Anishinabe Nation, White Earth, Minnesota. She is a freelance graphic designer, illustrator, and photographer and the owner of All Nite Design and Photography. Carly graduated from the College of Associated Arts in St. Paul with a B.A. in Communication Design. She lives in St. Paul.

Series Editor **Gordon Regguinti** is a member of the Leech Lake Band of Ojibway. He was raised on Leech Lake Reservation by his mother and grandparents. His Ojibway heritage has remained a central focus of his professional life. A graduate of the University of Minnesota with a B.A. in Indian Studies, Regguinti has written about Native American issues for newspapers and school curricula. He served as editor of the Twin Cities native newspaper *The Circle* for two years and is currently executive director of the Native American Journalists Association. He lives in Minneapolis and has six children and one grandchild.

Series Consultant **W. Roger Buffalohead**, Ponca, has been involved in Indian Education for more than 20 years, serving as a national consultant on issues of Indian curricula and tribal development. He holds a B.A. in American History from Oklahoma State University and an M.A. from the University of Wisconsin, Madison. Buffalohead has taught at the University of Cincinnati, the University of California, Los Angeles, and the University of Minnesota, where he was director of the American Indian Learning and Resources Center from 1986 to 1991. Currently he teaches at the American Indian Arts Institute in Santa Fe, New Mexico. Among his many activities, Buffalohead is a founding board member of the National Indian Education Association and a member of the Cultural Concerns Committee of the National Conference of American Indians. He lives in Santa Fe.

Series Consultant **Juanita G. Corbine Espinosa**, Dakota/Ojibway, serves as director of Native Arts Circle, Minnesota's first statewide Native American arts agency. She is first and foremost a community organizer, active in a broad range of issues, many of which are related to the importance of art in community life. In addition, she is a board member of the Minneapolis American Indian Center and an advisory member of the Minnesota State Arts Board's Cultural Pluralism Task Force. She was one of the first people to receive the state's McKnight Human Service Award. She lives in Minneapolis.